Black Cottonwood
Populus trichocarpa
H 60–125'; LV 2–8" L x
1.25–4.75" W

Quaking Aspen
Populus tremuloides
H to 50'; LV 1.25–3" L

Western Serviceberry
Amelanchier alnifolia
H 3–16'; LV 0.75–2" L

Kinnikinick
Arctostyaphylos uva-ursi
H to 6"; LV to 1"

Orange Honeysuckle
Lonicera ciliosa
L to 20'; F to 1.75"

Devil's Club
Oplopanax horridum
H 3–10'; LV 4–14" W

Blue Clematis
Clematis columbiana
H to 10'; F 0.75" L

Red Mountain Heather
Phyllodoce empetriformis
H 4–16"; LV 0.25" L

Alpine Laurel
Kalmia microphylla
H to 6"; LV to 0.75" L

Subalpine Spiraea
Spiraea densiflora
H 8–40"; LV to 1.5" L

Birchleaf Spiraea
Spiraea betulifolia
H 3–4'; F to 3.5" W

Yellow Mountain Heather
Phyllodoce glanduliflora
H to 12"; LV 0.25" L

Heartleaf Arnica
Arnica cordifolia
H 4–20'; LV 1–4" L

Yellow Columbine
Aquilegia flavescens
H 18–24"

Arrowleaf Balsamroot
Balsamorhiza sagittata
L to 12"; F 4–5" D

Mountain Buttercup
Ranunculus escholtzii
H to 8"; LV to 0.125" L;
F to 0.5" D

Roundleaf Violet
Viola orbiculata
H to 12"; LV to 2" L

Mountain Golden Pea
Thermopsis montana
H 12–48"; LV 2–4";
F 0.75–1" L

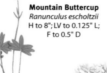

Lanceleaf Stonecrop
Sedum lanceolatum
H to 6"

American Globeflower
Troillus laxus
H 4–20"; F 1.5" D

Large Yellow Monkeyflower
Mimulus tilingii
H 2–4"; F 1" D

Yellow Fritillary
Fritillaria pudica
H to 1'; LV 1–8" L

Bracted Lousewort
Pedicularis bracteosa
H 8–20"

Orange Mountain Dandelion
Agoseris aurantiaca
H 4–24"; F 1" D

Tall Bluebell
Mertensia paniculata
H to 5'; LV 2–3" L

Common Harebell
Campanula rotundifolia
H 4–32"; F 0.75" L

Wood Forget-me-not
Myosotis sylvatica
H 6–18"; W 10–12"

Blue Camas
Camas camassia
H 12–24"; F 1.5–2" D

Silky Lupine
Lupinus sericeus
H to 6'; LV to 2.5" L

Common Blue-eyed Grass
Sisyrinchium idahoense
H 4–20"; F 0.5–1.5" D

Silky Phacelia
Phacelia sericea
4–24"; LV 1–4" L; F 0.25" D

Leafy Aster
Symphyotrichum cusickii
H to 4'; LV 2–5" L x 1.5" W

Explorer's Gentian
Gentiana calycosa
H 2–12"; LV to 1" L;
F 1–1.625" L

Sky Pilot
Polemonium viscosum
H to 3'; LV 2.5" L x 1" W

Showy Fleabane
Erigeron speciosus
H to 3'; W 1'

Upland Larkspur
Delphinium nuttallianum
H 4–7'

Glacier National Park includes trees and wildflowers from both the Northern Rockies and the Pacific Northwest. This card depicts many of the most common and some of the most beautiful trees and wildflowers that visitors are likely to encounter.

Alpine Aster
Oreostemma alpigenum
H 2–6"

Shrubby Penstemon
Penstemon fruticosus
H 6–16"; F 1–2" L

Blue Columbine
Aquilegia jonesii
H to 4"; F 1"

Fuzzytongue Penstemon
Penstemon eriantherus
H to 18"; LV 0.75" W

Pinesap
Hypopitys monotropa
H 2–10"

Coralroot Species
Corallorhiza species
H 8–32"; F 0.75" D

Common Butterwort
Pinguicula vulgaris
H 2–6"; LV 1–2" L; F to 1" L

Pinedrops
Pterospora andromedea
H 12–40"

Giant Helleborine
Epipactis gigantea
H 12–36"; LV 2–8" L;
F to 1.5"

Western Bronzebells
Stenanthium occidentale
H 4–20"; LV 4–12" L

THE MOUNTAINEERS BOOKS
1001 SW Klickitat Way, Suite 201
Seattle, WA 98134
mbooks@mountaineersbooks.org
www.mountaineersbooks.org
ISBN 1-59485-022-4
ISBN 13: 978-1-59485-022-6

ISBN 10: 1-59485-022-4

9 781594 850226   50595

Outdoor books by the experts

Subalpine Fir
Abies lasiocarpa
H 50–100';
C 2.25–4"

Engelmann Spruce
Picea engelmannii
H to 160'; C 2–3.5"

Grand Fir
Abies grandis
H to 290'; C 2–4"

Western Larch
Larix occidentalis
H to 260'; C to 1.5"

Douglas Fir
Pseudotsuga menziesii
H to 290'; C 2–3.5"

Western Hemlock
Tsuga heterophylla
H 100–160'; C to 1"

Western Red Cedar
Thuja plicata
H 150–200'; C 0.5"

Ponderosa Pine
Pinus ponderosa
H 150–180'; C 3–5.5"

Western White Pine
Pinus monticola
H 100–175'; C 5–9"

Whitebark Pine
Pinus albicaulis
H 20–50'; C 1.5–3.25"

Limber Pine
Pinus flexilis
H 30–50'; D 20"; C 3–6" L

Lodgepole Pine
Pinus contorta
H 30–90'; C 2.5"

Lyall's Rockcress
Arabis lyallii
H 4–10"; LV to 1" L x 0.25" W

Pink Dogbane
Apocynum androsaemifolium
H 8–20"; LV 1–2.5" L; F to 0.5" D

Twinflower
Linnaea borealis
H to 4"; LV to 1" L

Field Mint
Mentha arvensis
H to 2.6'; LV 4" L

Moss Campion
Silene acaulis
H 2–4.75"; F 0.5" D

Showy Milkweed
Asclepias speciosa
H to 6'; LV 6" L x 3" W

Fireweed
Epilobium angustifolium
H 3–10'; LV 3–6" L

**Rocky Mountain
Douglasia**
Douglasia montana
H 3"

Globemallow
Iliamna rivularis
H to 6.5';
LV 6–8" L & W

Alpine Fireweed
Epilobium alpinum
H to 8'

Elephantshead
Pedicularis groenlandica
H to 24"; LV 6" L

Sticky Geranium
Geranium viscosissimum
H 6–12"; LV 2–4" W

Pigmy Lewisia
Lewisia pygmaea
H to 4"; LV 1.5–6" L

Common Chokecherry
Prunus virginiana
var. *melanocarpa*
H to 20'; LV 2–4" L;
F 3–5" L

Common Beargrass
Xerophyllum tenax
H 2–5'; LV 6–24" L

Showy Green Gentian
Frasera speciosa
H to 4'; LV 4" L; F 0.75" D

False Hellebore
Veratrum viride
H 3–7'; LV 6–14" L x
3–6" W

Western False Solomon's Seal
Smilacina racemosa
H to 35";
LV to 7.5" L x 3" W

Pointed Mariposa Lily
Calochortus apiculatus
H 4–6"

Clasping Leaved Twisted Stalk
Streptopus amplexifolius
H 12–36"

Mountain Death Camas
Zigadenus elegans
H 6–28"; LV 6–12" L

Ladies Tresses
Spiranthes romanzoffiana
H 4–24"; LV 2–10" L

Alpine Lousewort
Pedicularis contorta
H 8–20"

Yampah
Perideridia gairdneri
H to 4'

Western Rattlesnake Plantain
Goodyera oblongifolia
H 6–16"; LV 3–7"

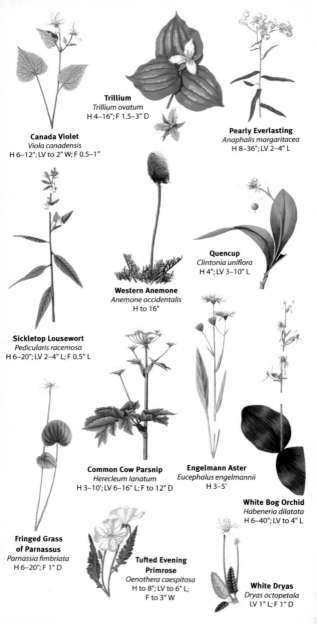

Trillium
Trillium ovatum
H 4–16"; F 1.5–3" D

Canada Violet
Viola canadensis
H 6–12"; LV to 2" W; F 0.5–1"

Pearly Everlasting
Anaphalis margaritacea
H 8–36"; LV 2–4" L

Quencup
Clintonia uniflora
H 4"; LV 3–10" L

Western Anemone
Anemone occidentalis
H to 16"

Sickletop Lousewort
Pedicularis racemosa
H 6–20"; LV 2–4" L; F 0.5" L

Common Cow Parsnip
Herecleum lanatum
H 3–10'; LV 6–16" L; F to 12" D

Engelmann Aster
Eucephalus engelmannii
H 3–5'

White Bog Orchid
Habeneria dilatata
H 6–40"; LV to 4" L

**Fringed Grass
of Parnassus**
Parnassia fimbriata
H 6–20"; F 1" D

**Tufted Evening
Primrose**
Oenothera caespitosa
H to 8"; LV to 6" L;
F to 3" W

White Dryas
Dryas octopetala
LV 1" L; F 1" D

Mock Orange
Philadelphus lewisii
H 5–15'; LV 12–20" L

Thimbleberry
Rubus parviflorus
H to 10'; LV 4–8" W

Red Osier Dogwood
Cornus stolonifera
H 6.5–20'; LV to 4.75" L

Alpine Wintergreen
Gaultheria humifusa
H 1.25"; LV 0.75" L

Cascade Mountain-ash
Sorbus scopulina
H to 80'; LV 3–6" L

Woods Rose
Rosa woodsii
H to 4'; F to 2.5" W

Shrubby Cinquefoil
Potentilla fruticosa
H 4–40"; LV 0.75" L

Labrador Tea
Ledum glandulosum
H to 6.5'; LV to 2" L

Red Raspberry
Rubus idaeus
H to 6.5'; F to 3.5" D

Red Elderberry
Sambucus racemosa
H 10–20'; LV to 6" L

Low Oregon Grape
Berberis repens
H 1–3'; LV 2" L

Creambush
Holodiscus discolor
H 1.5–10'; LV 1.5–3" L; F 4–7" L

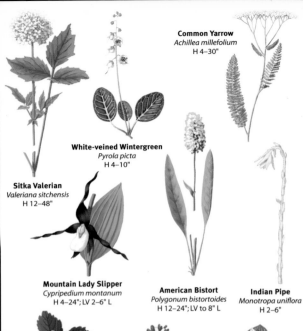

Common Yarrow
Achillea millefolium
H 4–30"

White-veined Wintergreen
Pyrola picta
H 4–10"

Sitka Valerian
Valeriana sitchensis
H 12–48"

Mountain Lady Slipper
Cypripedium montanum
H 4–24"; LV 2–6" L

American Bistort
Polygonum bistortoides
H 12–24"; LV to 8" L

Indian Pipe
Monotropa uniflora
H 2–6"

Broad-petaled Strawberry
Fragaria virginiana
H 3–6"; LV 1–2"

Hood's Phlox
Phlox hoodii
H to 2"; W to 10"

Bunchberry Dogwood
Cornus Canadensis
H 2–8"; LV to 3" L

Alpine Smelowskia
Smelowskia calycina
H 2–8"

Brown-eyed Susan
Gaillardia aristata
H 24"; W 24"

Glacier Lily
Erythronium grandiflorum
H 6–12"; LV 4–8" L